Sins and

Cigarettes

Makenna Misuraco

Acknowledgments:

To Jack Wild Publishing: For believing in my voice and giving me an opportunity to share it with the world.

To my parents: Thank you for showing me what true love is and that it does not alter. To never settle and that anything I want is possible, if I give it 150% of my heart.

To Jeff & Maddie: For not only being my siblings, but for being my people to go to when I feel like no one understands me.

To Alisa Verratti: My agent, my mentor, my life coach, and my best friend. This book would not have been possible without the role you have played.

To Carly: You have been the most consistent person in my life. You make me feel understood, seen, and heard. I will value the bond we have built for a lifetime.

To you: Thank you for inspiring me, for reading this, supporting me, and believing in me. You make me strong. You make me want to continue.

I love you all more than words on paper will ever due justice.

you won't read this,
but you inspired it.

To you I owe
all of my heartbreak,
my strength,
my determination,
and my success.

— Thank you.

Part I: For the Lovers

The thought of kissing you for the first time
brought me to my knees.

I spent hours engulfed in your conversation,
trying to keep up with the complexity of your brain-
while ignoring that time was still a factor in my life
and eventually this old city, upscale bar would close.

I'm not sure if it was the colder weather
or the remnants of vodka on your lips,
but I swear
the second we made contact,
you began to fill holes
that were home
to a broken interpretation
of love.

I remember rolling over

and looking at you while you were sleeping.

I wanted to wrap you in my arms,

so when you'd wake in the morning,

you would feel safe.

I couldn't touch you without ruining you,

so I didn't touch you at all.

It was 5:45 am.

Dawn was breaking

and the world that was dark,

suddenly had light again.

-You made me feel again that night.

Now that I know you're here,
existing the way you do—
It has been impossible
to look
at anyone
else.

You stole the cigarette from between my teeth
and took a seemingly endless drag.

I couldn't believe how jealous I was
at the thought of anything else against your lips.

I watched you inhale heavily
and became jealous of the smoke that filled your lungs,
as I craved to have that same ability
to take your breath away.

Use me as your fix,
put me between your fingertips.

Paint my life with chaos
and when you add in your finest details
be sure to use the warmest reds and the coldest blues.

When the ground rumbles from the sensation of your
hands grabbing my skin,
pull me closer and we'll watch the wind lose direction
from the pressure changing.

Kiss me with no regard of how we'll feel tomorrow,

      because tonight we'll chase

          the moon

      and scream our secrets

          to the stars.

There was *nothing*

more beautiful

than the sound

of her laugh

at 5am;

mixed with

bitter winter air

and tangled

bed sheets.

Through old, broken blinds and sore red eyes,
I stayed up to watch the sunrise over a small, vacant town.

You laid beside me
with your face buried into my neck
and I was in disbelief
at how I still wanted to pull you closer.

I worried about what morning would bring
and I feared that I'd wake up to an empty bed,
with only your outline present.

(I don't know how to tell you that
I have admired you more than any sunrise.)

Pull

     on

          my

             hips

until there are no spaces left

           between

       our

skin.

Darling,

I've been yours

right from

the start.

There was something
about the way that we made love;

          As if for years my bones had been broken,
              abandoned at a crossroad

and you drove all my lost pieces
          back home.

My words fell

     flat

when you questioned me:

     "What do I mean to you?"

If only I could have

opened up my hands

and held out the entire universe

with just the tips of my fingers.

     "You are everything."

And just like waves

kissing the shore line,

I have **no** control

over how hard I crash into you.

If these pages could talk

they would tell you how long I've been waiting

for someone like you

to come into my life.

If these pages could talk

they would say that

I'm afraid to write about being in love

because the universe might hear

that I'm happy

and take it away from me.

If these pages could talk

they would tell you how often

I write your name down

(And then scribble it out.)

I fell in love

with the way

that time

seems to exist

everywhere,

but between

us.

I have the world at my fingertips

and the only thing I want to feel

is you.

What if the sun and moon
were capable of loving one another,
but timing has never been quite right
for them to have a proper conversation?

There's something about her voice
that changes after 1 am.
It becomes soft.
Light.
Raspy.
She becomes more vulnerable
and willing to share her story
using the darkness of the night
to mask her fears about falling in love again.

I've become addicted to learning
these sides of her,
the ones that many aren't familiar with.
I will be mindful of them
and I will hold her gently;

On the mere chance
that she may hold me,
too.

And if I
could only have
one thing,
it would still be
you.

I have this memory of you, burned into my skull;

Even in this moment,

I can still hear the waves from the bay,

striking against the jetty.

Your hands felt like

warm water pouring out against my skin;

Enough to cleanse my tarnished heart,

but still leave me covered in chills.

Your silhouette stands at my bedroom door;

in the same spot

that I watched the moonlight kiss your face,

as you crawled up the bed and into my arms.

With this I learned that

    home is more than just a place

        where we reside at night.

It was the smile
that was exchanged only
through her light brown eyes
that reminded me that
this feeling
is what people exist for.

I need you to know that
I have been waiting for you.

    This is what I am here for.

I watch you bite the inside of your lip

and i can't tell you

how badly

I want to be the one

you sink your teeth into.

We watch lovers

become trends

and I can't help

but wonder

what this world

will make

of us.

She was so quick

to undo the buttons on her clothes

to satisfy me,

but what I wanted

could not be found

under

overpriced lace.

What I lusted for,

was her mind.

I craved to know what moves her.

The sun grazed her face
through my passenger side window.
My eyes drifted from the road
to admire the way it changed her hair
from black to light brown.
I had almost forgotten
that I was driving the car,
but in that moment,
it didn't seem to matter.

She had total control.

Promise to still love me

    when the music ends.

She has the ability

to stain my life with colors

that have never even existed.

I trace the freckles on your back
and watch as they bring life
to the most serene constellations,
creating a surge of light
throughout the room,
bright enough to set fire
to an entire city.

She didn't have to be pretty
like all of the other girls
she compared herself to.

What they had all lacked
was a passion strong enough
to make my bones feel less feeble.

Where as she
manifested enough
for both of us
to stand tall.

Talk to me
with your hands,
I'll take the time
to learn your language;

let the pressure
beneath your fingertips
say all the words
you choke on.

Your love runs through me like the blood in my veins.

How do I tell her
that I have barely slept since we met-
because sleeping means dreaming
in a dimension
that I may not find her in?

How do I tell her
that I have never been
a nervous person,
but every time she's near me
I become paralyzed?

I keep writing the words out,
but they don't make any sense.

(*This is how I'm telling her.*)

my heart aches for you
in the sweetest way.

My love language

can't be spoken in words

as simple as,

"you're pretty."

It can't be bought

in jewelry,

or flowers.

It won't be discovered

between my legs,

or within my bed sheets.

My love language

starts and ends at you

loving all of my flaws-

       accepting all of me.

We went our separate ways for quite some time
and in moments of vulnerability and fear of the world,
I found myself back with you
in the same bed where we first made love.

Those three days passed faster
than the time it took me
to say your name in an exhale,
but I know wherever we may move on to,
roads will always lead me right back to you.

I watched my addictions

walk through the doorway,

draped in black lace

accompanied by hazel eyes.

Therapy could not have prepared me

for the high I was

about to be engulfed in,

the second her lips

made contact

with my neck.

I'm a lightweight

for your touch,

and I'm drunk

off your lips

from one

taste.

Red has become such a frequent color in my mind.

It's the color of all extremes.

The highest and the lowest times of our lives.

Red can be love. Taking your heart and body into infinite dimensions. Red can be passion, drive, lust. An instant attraction. A first kiss. Red can be danger. A point where you shouldn't go any further. Red can be heat. Fire. Something that will burn your skin at the mere touch of it. Evil, lying, conniving and painful. Red can be fucking hell. Red can be hatred. The color you see in someone's eyes when they're angry or when they're spiteful. Raw, an open wound. Red can be bloody and messy, covering your hands until you're on the floor crying out for a higher power that you don't even believe in. Red can be beautiful, but at the same time a disaster waiting to unravel.

Passion. Fire. Danger. Hatred. Beauty. Love.

You are the color red to me.

I'm addicted to the way

your clothes look

lying across

my bedroom

floor.

It still feels like the first time.

You're always brand new.

I'm jealous of the people

who get to enjoy the sound

of your laugh

when I'm not around.

I promise
to be your rock
when life
makes you feel
like a sunken pit.

Perhaps-

the word

      beautiful

changed

after I saw you.

I saw our entire lives
at the brush of our first kiss.
I knew then,
that i could never know
a life without you.

(And i don't want to.)

Misuraco

Part II: For the Hurt

My back rested gently

against the rusted washing machine

in your Uncle's garage.

Whiskey lingered on your breath

and with your drunk lips

you kissed me hard.

It was twelve degrees that night,

but I was sweating.

      I didn't know who you would love

      when you woke up sober in the morning.

You hated the only song that ever made me feel alive.

-I should've known you were no good

As people,

we're programmed to believe

that loving too much

makes us weak.

When I first met you,

flowers blossomed throughout my resolve

whereas the seeds

hadn't even been planted

within yours.

Time carried on,

you tread in my dirt

and I realized

that you were the weak one

for being too scared

to love

anything at all.

We are caught in this vicious cycle
of falling in and out
of ourselves
and in and out
of each other.

Are we bad people

for smoking cigarettes-

knowing the consequences of our actions

will leave us wishing we had never taken

that initial drag?

Was I a bad person

for inhaling you-

while disregarding how much withdrawal I'd face,

when you'd no longer be mine?

Now,

I'm left wishing

that I had

never

put my lips

on either one.

You were the most beautiful version

of everything I feared.

Making the devil seem tasteful

as you'd set my skin on fire

with each individual touch.

I misread you for an angel,

but the Bible reminded me that even Lucifer

was once God's favorite.

It was hard to see through your glossy green eyes

and that crooked fucking smile,

but I wouldn't take it back.

> *Not even for a second.*

Cause for a while there,

you made hell feel like home.

You reminded me of whiskey.

How I took you in

smoothly

with zero hesitation,

but in the morning

felt the *worst* repercussions.

Many people have compared me to black coffee-

an acquired taste.

Sometimes, too bitter-

a little too harsh.

I took notice when she was pouring packets of sugar into

her coffee.

She hated the way it tasted when it was bitter

and didn't want to have to get used to the taste-

She didn't like the harshness.

-I just figured I wouldn't bother anymore.

The space where I used to hold you between my fingers

has been replaced with a nicotine stain.

One had the power to kill me

while the other was my choice,

but both burned *exactly* the same.

The biggest mistake I made
was allowing my heart
to become someone else's safe place.

I finally threw out the last t-shirt

you had left behind on my bedroom floor.

-I guess this is progress

No,
i dont think love can heal
our brokenness,
but we can try.

I didn't know the last time we kissed

would have been the

last time-

and now I wish I would've held you

for just a little bit longer.

Nostalgia has morphed

this perfect version of you inside my head.

Beauty embodied,

      soaked in innocence,

            drenched in grace.

I just have to remind myself that

      nostalgia is a dirty liar,

and so were you.

missing you comes in waves.

At times I'm still, feeling nothing at all.

other times,

    I'm

        fucking

           drowning.

Misuraco

Your hands left burn marks
the size of the sun on my skin
after you touched me.

Since then,
I've been on an expedition
around our solar system
to find a fix
for the gravitational force

that keeps pulling me
back to you.

Even in my most desperate attempts,

I could never be the

only one

to hold your attention.

You were a puppet master,
and I was a spineless entity
looking for a hand
to make me feel just a little

less empty.

This long drive has become a graveyard to my mind

    and the coffin where the memory of us was put to rest,

    has re-opened.

I expected to find the skeleton of what was,

    instead I found a mummy.

Perfectly persevered,

    as if there was a small hope it would come back to life.

We both know mummies aren't real,

    but they are a terrifying resemblance

    of something beautiful

    that once existed.

It's just one more reminder that

 what is gone might come back,

        but it will *never* be the same.

(b.m.)

It was almost pathetic,

the way that I would have rather been used by you

than loved

by someone else.

How do I heal myself

as quickly as you broke me?

They say it takes 21 days to break a bad habit.

The first 4 days is when you really feel the withdrawal.

It's day 1 without you and I've put 6 holes

in my bed room wall.

This means in 21 days,

I won't crave the feeling of your skin against mine.

In 21 days,

I'll no longer feel a tsunami arise in my stomach

when I hear your name.

21 days until I stop hearing your laughter echo

throughout my bones.

504 hours and I'll be able to sleep again.

30,240 minutes until I stop missing you.

1,814,400 seconds

and I won't be addicted to you anymore.

You set my entire world

on fire,

just to decide that you couldn't handle

the heat.

I lied to you

when I told you that I didn't love you anymore.

The truth was simple.

Your heart no longer lived in the same space as mine,

and you didn't have the guts to tell me.

You're an old flame,

I guess it's time

I let you

burn

out.

I didn't know that I could be so hungover
from consuming you recklessly,
but the temptation of your smile
had me hanging onto

      every

drunken word you slurred.

Our love was a chore

and you had to drag your feet

just to get by.

I wrote out your name

with lines of cocaine

in hopes to see which of the two

could make me feel

more numb.

You told me that I would never find
 someone like you again.

That no one could love me
the way you did,
again.

While this may have been true,
what you didn't know
was how badly I looked forward to it.

I never knew that I could feel the color black

until I told her I would always love her

    and silence

        kissed me back.

I refuse to be sorry for how I chose to mend
what *you* broke.

I could have carried my love for you
through the front lines-
through one thousand wars.

I could have carried my love for you
through the front lines-
I let my blood keep you warm
on nights when you had no home.

But you took all my ammunition
and claimed my safe house as
your battle ground-
trampling my heart in the process.

I tried to surrender,
but you were taking
no prisoners

(a.v.)

I feel like I have met you
in one hundred different lifetimes.

(I wonder if any of them ever got it right.)

I've been having these moments where I'm driving in the car and my mind starts to replay all of the little things. I'm no longer focused on what color the traffic light is, using my blinker, or hitting my breaks.

It's the way you'd kiss the back of my hand when we were driving late at night. It's you coming up behind me and hugging my waist. It's the holidays and your laughter. It's us out to dinner and you winking at me from across the table. It's the cold winter air cracking our lips, but you kissing me hard anway. It's the smell of your hair fresh out of the shower. It's you rolling over in the middle of the night and pressing your tired mouth against my forehead.

It's the way you looked at me- that changed everything.

I should probably pump the breaks,

but the little things keep me going.

Oh,

how lucky she must be

to be the one

who feels your gaze.

And i realized

    i struggled more in your presence

than i ever did in your absence.

It wasn't until
10 consecutive months
of drinking whiskey
straight,
that I realized
I was searching for you
at the bottom
of every bottle.

I poisoned myself
with every cheap sip,
so I could stop
seeing you in everything
and feeling you in everyone.

I know they say time heals all wounds,

but for me,

the whiskey worked *just fine.*

You made all of the plans

    and eventually I forgot my own.

In a perfect world

where timing is always in our favor,

I invariably find my way back to you.

But in this world,

you are just a name

that my heart *continuously* bleeds out for.

I am able to find your lips

amongst the different faces I meet

and though I may get my fix from them,

        they will never taste quite like you.

This vodka is strong enough to remind me

that we still live in the same city,

and if I am able to convince my drunk feet

to keep up with my sober heart,

then eventually I'll find myself standing at your doorstep.

-I just need to focus

I talked about you
until I was blue in the face,
and the moment my lips
stopped speaking your name,
my lungs couldn't find
any more air to breathe.

It doesn't matter that you're gone.

I'll love you through the distance.

I remember the day that I started looking at you differently.

Your hands felt foreign

and the smell of your skin was unfamiliar.

You were no longer this bright light

that could make me feel safe.

No, what we had was never ideal,

and it was always toxic,

but it was **ours**.

With my temptations

come hesitations

and trust issues

as a result of

your selfish tendency

to never sleep at home.

Each time we make eye contact,

I feel the lies you fed me

fill up my throat

and crawl across my tongue,

until I am practically choking

on every last bit of false hope

for you to turn back into the person

I thought I once knew.

For the times
that you were able to throw me away
like I was trash,

crumple me up and toss me
across the room,

without gaining a single papercut
on your precious hands,

just to later on
mail cardboard boxes
full of empty apologies.

I still wonder why I kept taking you back,
to just be used again.

-your recycled "love"

Your fingers skimmed the outline of my body
while your eyes trailed alongside them;
following each individual goosebump they created against
my skin.
I knew you were taking in that moment
and embedding the memory of our untainted love into your
skull,
so you could remember what you walked away from
when the next person you have disappoints you.

Remember me on Monday mornings
when you wake up to work your typical 9-5 desk job
and you search for a thrill at the bottom of your coffee cup.
Remember me on your 5th smoke break
that you'll chief down in hopes for a momentary head high.
When you get home, have dinner by yourself and drink
enough liquor to feel better about going to bed alone,
remember when you told me,
"this was fun while it lasted."

Sins & Cigarettes

And in every war
I'd surrender
the second you called me,
"baby."

102

There are moments in the middle of the night

where I wake up and want to scream,

but my vocal chords are being strangled by two fists

that are stronger than my will to live.

So I swallow the sounds

and learn to stomach the thought

of what you and I

could have been,

and force myself back to sleep.

In your eyes,

holding onto your ego

was far more important

than holding on to me.

I'm sorry for the way that I left.
With no explanation.
For not answering your calls.

If we're being honest,

I was too weak to hear your voice
on the other end of the phone.

(I still am)

I hate to admit

that a part of my soul

will forever be put to the side

with your name

written across it

in case you decide to come back someday.

I would wait for the nights

that you would get

drunk enough to slip up and say,

"I love you."

I have felt the weight of missing you

hit me from *every* angle

and though you were never consistent,

I still rolled with your punches.

Your intentions may not have been to have

such a heavy fist,

but I can't remember the last time

I've been so beaten

      that I became numb.

She may not have been the best for me,

but she wasn't the worst either.

And it was just enough to make the time without you

pass by

a little faster.

What we had wasn't a fairytale by any means ,

so I hope it doesn't seem that way

through the words I pour out for you.

In fact,

the only commonality is

that it was all make believe.

My heart aches less to think that maybe you miss me too.

When she clutches the sheets

on your bed with her fists

and moans out your name

at the sound of her release,

do you wish it were me?

-I do.

I hated you

for not loving me back,

but I hated myself *even more*

for agreeing

with every reason

why you didn't.

This whiskey goes down like water

and makes the lips of a stranger

taste like yours.

When you find yourself in a haze
and you think of me,
please know that I do not miss you.
I never wonder how you are
or how your day has been.
I don't remember how you take your coffee,
your favorite flower,
or who your favorite band is.
I don't remember your smell,
or how your lips feel against mine.

When you think of me,
remember that I am lying to myself.

(Cream, no sugar.
Sunflowers.
Chicago.
Lavender.
Home.)

I've become comfortably numb to the thought of you in someone else's arms.

I can't sleep,

but I'll dream of what we could be.

A little bit of liquor
and she's falling in love with
the first person
to give her attention.

I'm in love
with the moon,
freshly cut grass,
and the way the pavement smells after
it has rained.

And you, of course.
You.

I'm in love
with worn out,
hardcover books,
dusty vinyls,
and cities compacted with 2 million people.

And you, of course.
You.

The list continues of things I love,
that will never be capable
of loving me back.

Like you, of course.
You.

I Remember you
in all of your most beautiful forms.

No matter what we are now,
and regardless of who we become,

I will always remember
what we were.

Misuraco

Part III: For the Past

I feel like a foreigner
in a place
that I have lived
      my entire life.

I am proud of you for not crumbling

when your world and all of the people in it

told you that you couldn't be who you are.

"I am so scared for you."
My mother cries out with tears in her eyes,
realizing that I am not capable of loving
the gender I'm supposed to.

But do not be afraid, Mom.
You raised me to be strong.
To never give up.
To go after everything that I want.
You taught me love
and happiness.

And now I will *finally* have it.

I found my heart caught in a game of
tug of war;

between projecting my love
for every soul to hear,

or swallowing it down with a liquor
that makes me a stranger to feeling.

You fear not enough people seeing you
while I fear too many people seeing me.

All of these beatdowns

have left my ribs

black and blue,

and my chest so sore.

My memory

no longer knows the difference

between making love

and pure lust,

or being in love

and being full of hatred.

-Fine Lines

Tonight I'll drink.

And I'm not quite sure why..

A memory that needs forgetting.

A touch that needs numbing.

I'll drink for the father who is 8 months sober,

on the verge of giving in.

I'll pour one out for the girl who can't shake the thought

of his aggressive, unlawful hands beneath her skin.

I'll toast to the people in their lonely hours,

who only remember empty promises and resentful words.

I keep thinking about you.

Wondering where you are.

So tonight,

I'm drinking to forget you.

I reached out my hand to grab darkness by the throat ,

in hopes to make it feel smaller

than my fears.

But the fire that's been dormant in me for so long, sparked,

turned the lights on,

and told me to move forward.

I try to take things one day at a time,
but lately
I've slept the sun away
while dreaming
I could wake up
as someone else.

I will always be right here,

waiting to be seen by you.

You can try to paint over me,

but I will be the *only*

       permanent thing left

when the rain comes

          to wash it all

            away.

For years I spent my time thinking

that the love I receive from others

is ultimately what will define me.

But at the peak of my isolation,

I discovered that I wasn't such bad company,

and all beautiful things have the ability

to flourish alone.

I learned true loyalty and trust

when I stopped falling for the fabricated words

people spit out at me to shut me up.

Instead, I began to watch and observe

their actions and behaviors,

to assure myself that

they were inconsistent

all throughout.

I've always enjoyed the idea of the beach
      more than I actually liked being there.

      The last time I went to see the ocean,
      the wind knocked the life out of me

      and triggered me back to the time you told me
      I wasn't what you thought you wanted, after all.

Learning to trust again

    is not so simple.

    You see,

    houses crumble faster

        than they can be rebuilt.

Feeling butterflies in your stomach

is not endearing.

It is the bodies way of saying:

"Slow down, this might be dangerous."

One step

      is all it takes

      for me to move forward,

      but I'm not sure if I can handle

the weight of this world anymore.

I can feel the anxiety

seeping into my skin

and stopping me from breathing,

until I am a prisoner

of its every move.

      But,

         it's only one step.

I've loved so many people wrong
because i didn't know how to love myself right.

I hope that at the end of each day

you fall asleep knowing

you are enough.

You are so loved.

I wonder how many versions of you

this world will see

until you are finally

      yourself.

I search through every clock,
hoping to find hands
with enough minutes to spare me.

Will there ever come a time
that I can stain
someone's life permanently?

Will anyone ever take the time
to understand me-
hold me gently?

I'm not sure what I'm waiting for.

I hope that it's you.

If density forces us to sink in water,

how do we learn to stay afloat?

I spent years

building brick walls

around myself for protection,

that when it came time to

tear them down,

there was a stranger standing

on the other side.

I watch men and women walk hand in hand

without a care in the world.

People often approach them,

with compliments like,

"You two make such a lovely couple."

I walk the same streets

hand in hand

with the person that

I love

and receive nothing more than dirty looks

and insults such as,

"Fags."

It's a weird feeling.

The moment you realize

no one actually knows you.

When all that's known

is the version of yourself

you chose to give away.

You let others make their own assumptions,

and create their own perception of you.

Even if it's all a lie.

I know they've got it all wrong.

Is it even worth defending myself?

I hope you reach a point in your life
where you stop expecting people to
always give you second chances.

"So, what? What happens if I fall in love with you?"

-Don't

Why should I believe in your promises?

I would be a damn fool

to fall for the same script again.

(Do promises even mean a thing anymore?)

My story is more
than the nightmare i shared with you.
I just haven't found a way to tell it
without your name resurfacing.

- one day.

I hid my fears

using other people's bodies,

but all of my demons

still looked

like you.

Every time you called me yours,

I seemed to forget that I am

    only

        m i n e.

I have always struggled

with being alone,

but I am never surprised

that no one stays.

I confessed my dreams to you

with tears in my eyes,

as we pinky promised

that we would take it all on

together.

I am only one sip away

from tasting everything

that I've wanted,

but you're not here

like you once swore you would be.

(And there are still tears in my eyes.)

2 am

I'm on *another*

blackout binge again,

searching for the same security

I found in the sound of your fist

hitting our bedroom wall.

I used to get high

off of the way you used me,

and now I'm left longing for hands

that will entice me

the same exact way.

Maybe in another life
I'll get away with
holding your hand in public
or kissing you whenever, just because I can.
In an ideal world,
we can do this without people staring
as they wonder how disappointed
our families must be.

For now,
I'll take the dirty looks and people glaring.
I'll stomach the comments and the hand gestures,
because deep down I know
that the people who can't sleep
over those of us who love the same gender,
are really the ones
who are so unhappy
with themselves.

Lately my mind is becoming

my own worst enemy,

bound together by denial

and waves of ecstasy.

I'm struggling to find faith

beneath the barriers of my walls.

They are both my greatest legacy

and the key to my downfall.

Your ghost brushes gently against my lips

and though you aren't present,

I feel you wrapped around my hips.

Now at night I walk alone

on these dark empty streets,

searching for something to stop my hands

from trembling with fear and defeat.

I wear my scars to tell the story

of how I self inflicted

in hopes to release you

from underneath my skin.

Years later,

I look down at them,

and I don't feel your grip

on my wrists anymore.

These scars,

I wear them to remind myself,

that I can make it through another day.

You showered me with gifts,

but silenced me with your fists,

making sure I stayed aware

that you would always have

the upper hand.

I am damaged beyond fixing,

but I would patch up every wound

with bandaids

if it meant that I could

trick myself into believing

that I'm okay

just as easily as I have fooled

everyone else.

The darkness of your eyes

was deeper than any ocean

I had come to face.

It was funny,

how clearly I could see

my own reflection in them,

but not recognize myself at all.

-At some point I started drowning in your waters,

but still hoped you'd teach me how to swim.

Remember how we forgot.

"I am not gay.

How could I be gay?

I wasn't raised this way."

I say to myself as I let her kiss my neck

and throw me onto her bed.

I have a collection of unfilled voids

        and a diary of unsaid words.

Both stay stored away in my closet,

alongside the skeleton of you.

I watched a young girl

fall in love with the world,

no matter how evil

or unfair.

It inspired me,

how much of her heart she gave,

regardless of the fact

that she may never

be given anything back in return.

       -Why aren't we taught

            to love one another like that?

Please don't hate your parent's for not understanding you.

They *were not* taught better.

We do still have an opportunity

to change the way they view things.

Be vocal,

be patient,

teach them.

Continute to love them.

My triggers alert my anxiety,

"Wake up, it's time to go."

I struggle with 13 minutes of pure torture,

as my internal organs begin to switch places.

My heart falls to my stomach,

my stomach to my feet,

while my lungs hunt for any oxygen at all.

I wrestle with myself to regain control,

because I know my mind

is only playing tricks on me.

So I begin screaming

to my own brain,

"Wake up, it's time to go."

I still Remember being 16 -
lying on the couch in my mother's basement,
screaming into pillows,
while searching for an answer
to fill the void in my chest.

" How is my heart so heavy
    When i still have so much left to learn,
                so much left to feel?"

I know in this moment
someone is out there questioning it all.

Hear me:
        there is so much more to life
                and it's all waiting for you to arrive.

Part IV: For the Future

Don't just fall in love
with temporary things.

Fall in love with yourself,

for it will be the only thing
you get to keep.

Educate and breathe life into the upcoming generations;

Do not shut them down.

Give them the choice to make a life they want.

A life they are proud of.

People change.

we grow apart.

It is okay.

Even if it doesn't now,

everything will make sense.

The world is too big

and the universe is far too powerful

for things to only be a coincidence

or happen by chance.

In this exact moment,

       we are exactly where we are meant to be.

Why do we stop ourselves

    from saying words as simple as:

        "I love you."

            "Please stay."

                "I am sorry."

There is delicacy,

    and beauty,

to how vulnerability ignites our fears.

Our ability to create

is *limitless.*

Let your curiosities tempt you to take chances
that you never imagined you would take.

There's a lot to be said for the people who want to make you laugh on good days and even harder on the bad ones. Who stay up at all hours of the night to listen, simply because they care. Who push you to succeed and support any task you take on, no matter how difficult or out of reach. Who remain constant and stable while the rest of the world is ignited with mayhem. The people who help you back onto solid ground, when life feels like giving up.

The people who never stop loving, giving or fighting;

no matter the cost.

What is it that separates us as individuals?
What breaks us as a society?
We think we're so different from one another,
but at the end of the day,
all we are is
flesh
on *bone*
waiting to see what life has in store for us.
We all just want to hear someone say,

"Relax, everything is going to be okay."

I play all of my favorite sad songs
when I'm the happiest in my life,
to see how the words I resonated so deeply with a few
months back, feel in present day.
It helps me reflect on my growth as a human being and re-
minds me that even the worst type of pain is just a temporary
fleeting feeling.

There is not enough time

for mediocre sex

or to miss the people

who never think twice about you.

It disappoints me that as a society,
we have been bred
to pass judgements
because it's "easier"
to hate something
than to try to understand it.

Love shouldn't have to wait in line.

There is one thing that will ultimately stand in the way
of every dream in life;
Love.
Success.
Happiness.

     That one thing,
         is you.

There is nothing wrong
with walking away from something toxic,
even if you relapse a few times
as you stumble out the door.

I pRay for my son
oR daughteR;
that they don't have to
hesitate
to hold the hand
of the peRson they love.

We are nothing more
than herds of sheep
fleeing from wolves,
doing everything we can
to ensure survival.

Note to self:

Happiness may seem like a far fetched,
out of reach idea,
but let go of assuming
where your life should be right now.

Great things take time,
It took Michelangelo *four years*
to paint the Sistine Chapel.

Love is not a game of possession.
It is not holding the other hostage,
or claiming your territory.

Love is selfless.
> Unguarded.
>> Sacred.

None of us have any idea what we're doing,
some people are just better at hiding it.

-I call bullshit

It's never Really oveR until the second you stop tRying.

Just because people stand in the same circle as you,

doesn't mean they're in your corner.

Bad tongues talk,

but the good ones

will make

your legs

      shake.

I've always tried to be something more.

More loving.

More graceful.

More understanding.

More valuable.

More perfect.

But I realized

I can't be more

and no matter how much I give,

at the *very* most

I will only be human.

Jealousy isn't what you see,

it's what you imagine.

Never let the person you love

fall asleep angry.

Remind them how much

they mean to you.

And do it often.

Swallow your pride-

Be a better you.

Be with someone

who makes you feel

like being 1 of 8 billion people

means

something.

We can laugh at the confusion

and call what we've built

"accidental"

but nothing has made more sense

or been so clear.

(It almost makes me think it is our purpose.)

Don't spend too much time
fixated on things
you don't have the power
to change.

Stop moving miles for people

who won't even move an inch for you.

As children,

It's so easy for us to believe

in fictional characters,

but as time goes on

we forget how to believe

in ourselves.

It's hard not knowing

where roads ahead of us might lead-

but sometimes

fate does you favors

and drives you to a place

so unimaginably beautiful.

I want to show the Real me.
I want to be transparent
and unafraid that if i show too much,
you'll leave.

Let me show you
where i cry from,
and allow you to shake hands
with my insecurities.

I want you to love
all of the madness,
because,
though it took me so long,

     I finally do.

Made in the
USA
Columbia, SC